Letter from my Foster Mother

and other stories

Short story collections available from Evertype

Letter from my Foster Mother and other stories
(Fionntán de Brún, tr. Mícheál Ó hAodha 2020)

The Scarlet Petal and other stories
(Ryan Petrie 2020)

The Book of Poison (Panu Petteri Höglund & S. Albert Kivinen,
tr. Colin Parmer & Tino Warinowski 2014)

The Partisan and other Stories (Gabriel Rosenstock,
tr. Mícheál Ó hAodha & Gabriel Rosenstock 2014)

A Nosegay of Pleasant Delights: Five-minute fictions (Brian S. Lee 2012)

The Burning Woman and other stories (Frank Roger 2012)

Neighbours: Stories in Mennonite Low German and English
Nohbasch: Jeschichte opp Plautdietsch enn Enjlisch
(Jack Thiessen 2014)

Nosy Neighbours: Stories in Mennonite Low German and English
Nieschieaje Nohbasch: Jeschichte opp Plautdietsch enn Enjlisch
(Jack Thiessen 2015)

Letter from my Foster Mother

and other stories

by

Fionntán de Brún

Translated from the Irish by

Mícheál Ó hAodha

evertype

2020

Published by Evertype, 19A Corso Street, Dundee, DD2 1DR, Scotland.
www.evertype.com.

First published in Irish by Móinín, Baile Uí Bheacháin, 2005, with the title
Litir ó mo Mháthair Altrama agus Scéalta Eile. ISBN 0-953277-77-1.

Text © 2005 Fionntán de Brún.
Translation © 2020 Mícheál Ó hAodha.

First edition 2020.

A catalogue record for this book is available from the British Library.

ISBN-10 1-78201-267-2
ISBN-13 978-1-78201-267-2

Set in Minion Pro and Étienne by Michael Everson.

Cover: Michael Everson.
Cover photograph "Train at Connolly Station - (13)" © The Carlisle Kid –
cc-by-sa/2.0 – geograph.org.uk/p/3252050.

Contents

Letter from my Foster Mother

and other stories

Letter from my Foster Mother

You were born on the 12th of June 1953, a fine sunny day in early-summer. I was looking out the window of a train that day on the most fertile lands ever seen and on patches of scattered silver where the dew had gathered on the grass. It was like a new and golden time that day where everything dingy and grey looked bright—the back streets of East Belfast, black with smoke and soot; it was one of those days when even the most worn-out tramp seemed reborn despite themselves. It was as if the whole world had an inkling that you were on the way; the people out shopping for things in the city, the workers in the fields gathering hay; all I saw was their bright and joyous faces quietly congratulating me that my time had finally come. Everything I saw and heard that day was like a sign that this was the pinnacle, my day of all days, the day my luck had finally come.

I nodded off after a while with the gentle jouncing of the train. I'd had a long night and a broken sleep. And I dreamed of everything that happened the previous year—all the different things. About meeting

Ned and all the work I'd done on the back room getting ready for your arrival. As usual, Ned wasn't much help with the preparations, he never stuck long at anything. And as sure as God, while I was in painting the walls, his hand was in my purse swiping whatever few pound he could—and I never saw it again afterwards.

The train was pulling into Dundalk when I woke up and the customs people came aboard. I leaned back in my seat and stared out the window. Ned couldn't help himself. He was weak the same as all the men I've ever known. Then again, maybe it was me who was weak seeing as I'd taken on the likes of Ned in the first place. I certainly hadn't followed my mother's lead anyway; she was a woman who'd put manners on any man. I often wept at night thinking of her standing in the kitchen kneading bread with those big strong fingers of hers, the slow, regular rhythm of her powerful blue-veined hands.

I saw little enough of the countryside between Dundalk and Dublin that day, I was so tired. So much the better of course, seeing as once I walked out of the station in Dublin my heart was pounding. The big shuffling crowds and all of them strangers. I didn't know a soul and they didn't know me. I'd made a small rule for myself on the way down—I'd say nothing to anyone that day—if I could help it at all. I had the hours of the trains off backwards and written down on a scrap of paper just in case. And if I took that paper out and stared at it once that day, I stared at it a hundred times. I travelled light and didn't even bother with food. I'd no hunger for it.

I can't remember now what I did for that first half-hour I spent in Dublin. I wandered around aimlessly, clueless as to where I was going, breathless with excitement. And the heat that day was like a great crushing weight! Only that I went into a public toilet and got a drink from the tap I'd have collapsed in a heap on the street. By the time I reached Parnell Street, I was in a right state. I checked the time and realized I'd only about half-an-hour left. I began to panic. What if I didn't get you at all and I went home again on the train that evening empty-handed—on my own!

Then, as if in a trance, I saw you there suddenly in front of me! In your pram outside the chemist's shop—lying there quietly—your eyes wide-open, all new to the world. I walked towards you slowly so that I could enjoy the wonder that awaited me in all its fullness. I pulled back the canopy to get a proper look at you and to smell that lovely baby-clothes' smell of you up close. I'd love it if you could only understand the feeling of pure joy and longing that filled me in that moment when you grabbed hold of my finger for the first time ever. There's no treasure in the world like a new baby, so pure and sweet, and soul-unblemished.

There wasn't a peep out of you as I lifted you out of your pram. Walking back to the station with you in

3

my arms, I was in heaven. People must have noticed
us making our way through the crowds and along the
streets, me laughing and tripping over myself with
happiness and you in my arms staring intently up at
me all the while. It was ten-to-3 when we reached the
station, enough time to buy cigarettes. The woman in
the shop paid you great attention—needless to say—
a beautiful baby and a delighted new mother. Who
wouldn't have noticed us that afternoon?

"What's his name?"

I stuttered. I wanted to say Mark but "Mike" came
out. She laughed. I snatched the change from her
hand and off we went down the platform to the train.
I started to settle down as I sat into the carriage,
smoking a quick fag, and putting that bitch out of my
mind. I remember the powerful sense of peace that
came over me, something I'd never felt before as the
rays of the evening sun touched my forehead and me
thinking of how the whole of our lives awaited us and
how it was ours now to make the best of it. Where to
begin? What first pleasure awaited us? Joy overcame
me in great waves, making my head light. I couldn't
sit still such was the ecstasy of that moment.
Eventually I got up and walked the length of the train
and back again to try and settle down. I went down
the narrow passageway and the pins and needles alive
with every step as I covered your eyes from the
blinding light when the train emerged from a tunnel.
And that look that came over you—that look that

young children have when they know you're protecting them from something they cannot understand.

But when you leave one train carriage it's never easy to return to the same spot you were sitting in before and I sat into a different carriage on my return, one that had a woman and a boy in it already. I don't understand how things work out this way—that you find yourself in the wrong place at the wrong time or someone arrives into your life at a particular moment in time—or leaves you as unexpectedly again. The same as my mother and Ned both left me. I had that feeling the minute I passed into the wrong carriage that evening however. I still curse the moment that I got up and left our seat in the first place instead of enjoying the drunken joyous dream for what it was. No sooner had I stepped through the door of this new carriage but I felt the hope and joy drain out of me. And then I looked up at the pair sitting opposite me, examining us—you and me—as brazen as you like, and without the slightest hint of embarrassment. The mother was one of them that thinks she has the right to stare at strangers. She stared and she stared and the son the same way, a young lad of about 10 years of age, fascinated all of a sudden at this strange *specimen* that had appeared in front of him—like he was studying a spider or a beetle in a jar.

To stop them staring, I tried to play them at their own game and so I looked slowly from one of them to the other trying my best to shame them into looking in the other direction—but I was wasting my time. Eventually I sat down and stared straight at the mother—straight into the big nosy head of her. It was you who broke the silence however. You began to cry. You were hungry needless to say and I had no way of feeding you. I did whatever I could to soothe you and relax you in the hope that you'd have a short snooze for yourself but you didn't. If we'd been alone, you'd have fallen asleep no bother but it was impossible with this pair in front of us, their faces stuck in ours and their curiosity burning a hole through us all the while. When I looked up at the boy he had placed his hands over his ears at the sound of your cry, a big mischievous grin on his face. The mother gave him a nudge but the truth was she was proud of her young lad's cheek.

You got tired in the end and your eyes began to droop and fade until you fell into a heavy sleep. I don't know how I managed it at all but I didn't budge or leave my seat for the rest of the journey in case you woke up and you gave that aching cry of yours. I ignored the puddle of sweat that I was sitting in, my blouse stuck to my back, hot then cold. I knew that I'd be strong enough when I had to be and I felt angry now at these two and the ignorant stares of them. I gave the frumpy old heap opposite me a contemptuous look, with her cheap hat and the little greasy curls hanging out of it. Her like wasn't to be feared and I started up a conversation just to show it.

I asked her what she was in Dublin for but she didn't bother with a reply and instead a flood of questions came back at me. About the baby. What age were you? Were you more like your dad? Did you have any brothers and sisters at all? Did you sleep at night? That old feeling came back straight away, like I was fading away and all alone in the world, same as before.

The train began to slow and people gathered up their luggage and got ready for the last stop. I felt my stomach heave against the movement of the train pulling in. I'd wait until the crowd eased off. But the woman was still there beside me asking me a million questions. What about the pram and could she help me, and had I anyone there to meet me? I left the train in the end and even after all that, you never cried once.

I don't like to think about the rest of that day. You know yourself anyway and if you were to dig out the papers for that week you'd get a full report of everything—one of the passengers on the train that afternoon was suspicious of a woman who had a young baby with her but no sign of a bottle, a blanket, or even a bag. This inquisitive passenger decided to follow the woman and see where she was going. As I say, the rest of the story is yours.

How the Author Died

The more time you spend in a pub or a café the less you believe in time itself—after a couple of hours, clocks and watches cease to have any meaning. Having spent most of the day in a café in Montparnasse, I realized that I'd need to leave if I were to catch the last train. All that remained of the day's customers were two couples who, having nothing to say, sat rigidly staring ahead, in a timeless stupor. This was encouragement enough to face the outside world and then to cross the street without looking for traffic, wondering all the while about the one great timetable to which every city submits. Hurrying along the pavement, I took care to skip over the black slush that would fill my canvas shoes with the iciest of cold water. Under the brass arch of the métro station I stopped and listened for the sounds below, as the final groans became a death rattle and then a vast silence.

Perhaps I had no part in it, perhaps I missed the train because of an internal clock in all of us that governs even the time spent in pubs, constantly turning over, recording and directing us according to its desire. I had returned to the same café at any rate, a little busier and with no sign of the couples. The crowd that had come in were night workers, people who wanted to postpone the long night ahead just a little bit. Of course they paid no attention to me, knowing that I belonged to a different "frequency" and that we would have little in common. One person, however, did speak to me. Firstly, it was to ask for a cigarette. Then he stood with me for a while, intending, as I presumed, to give me a cigarette's worth of conversation in return. But he wanted more cigarettes, one after the other. Eventually I had to pretend that I didn't have a second packet in my coat pocket. "I'm sorry. Perhaps one of your friends has a cigarette?"

I realized then that he was alone, like myself. I opened the packet and gave him a cigarette, warning him that his death would be on my conscience if he smoked too many of them.

"I don't think you'll be with me when that happens," he replied, "besides, I might never get one of those diseases, they don't get everyone."

He must have noticed me becoming impatient with the conversation. I was certainly doing my best to ignore him, hoping that I might be left with even one or two cigarettes. The only thing left to do was to will the café and all of its customers into some kind of a time-trough and escape it for a while. But he was there all the while, smoking my cigarettes and shifting from one foot to the other, remaining always a yard or two from me or right up beside me. Then, without warning, he sidled up as though about to kiss me.

"Do you know—*could you tell*," he whispered, "that I am a murderer?"

He filled his throat with smoke and started to cough. His eyes were full of tears and his head turned away slightly with the coughing, yet he kept one eye on me expecting some sort of an answer.

"Shocking, don't you think?"

"I don't know. There are murderers and those who have murdered. Which are you?"

"Perhaps I should say that I am a 'literary murderer', in that I killed a writer."

"Do you mind if I ask who, or is that confidential?"

"Not at all. I killed a man whose work is held in libraries all over the world, a man who has been a hero to thousands, millions perhaps. He has been my hero ever since."

He stopped momentarily as his voice began to catch.

"I am the man who killed Roland Barthes."

"Roland Barthes?" I repeated, laughing incredulously.

"I thought Barthes was run over by a van of some sort."

"He was," he answered. "I was driving the van."

There was a look in his eyes that demanded pity rather than mockery and so, as though handling a holy shroud, he took out his wallet and carefully revealed a newspaper cutting within its folds. It was brown with age and had been reduced to four precariously-thin squares. He gave me time to read it, staring intently at me all the while, before showing me his driving licence for further proof.

"What do you think?" he asked.

"I'm surprised you're still allowed the licence," I replied.

He didn't respond but turned to order us two glasses of beer. Now it was my turn to be beholden to him, not having the money to pay for the drinks.

"I'm sure I don't envy you," I started, "I don't have a car but if I knocked someone down I'd say I'd—"

"I couldn't get it out of my head," he said slowly, interrupting.

"The noise his body made against the van. It was sudden, vulgar—oafish even. All of the things the great man was not."

"Did you know him?" I asked.

"No—no, until then I had never laid eyes on him. But I have got to know him very well through his books since." With that, he raised his glass in his honour.

"I don't know why he crossed my path like that, but all I know is that it was the equivalent of the *big bang* in my life—if I can say that. When I stepped out of that van to look at him it was like stepping into another world, a world in which I was a complete stranger.

"My marriage was the first thing to go. That awful noise never left my ears for months afterwards—I couldn't sleep with it. I just couldn't lie at peace in bed. I understood completely when my wife threw me out—she really had no option. The biggest thing any couple have to do is sleep together. Eight hours lying together every single night! Thinking about it now, I don't know how people do it. But once you begin to disrupt a couple's sleep, it's only a matter of time.... She has a new man now who sleeps like a baby. My job in the laundry was the next thing to go, but I wasn't fired. I left the laundry of my own volition. It was after reading an article by the great man himself—about washing powder—that I knew I was only wasting my time in the place.

"Every word of his that I read was a revelation. Of course, it wasn't easy reading to begin with, what with me never having really read anything much before that. But I gradually came to realize that this society we live in is founded on myths and illusions and that we are like sleepwalkers who may never wake up. After that, I couldn't see the world as I'd seen it before—everything I saw was passed through the filter that I had been granted by the great man. Even wrestling! Those men you see on television, roaring and brawling like mad children—it was only when I read an article the great man had written, that I understood these wrestlers are really gods, the key that releases our true nature so that we can separate

13

good from evil and the purity of justice is as a revelation to us. Imagine explaining that to your friends! The likes of me who was always one of the lads, and now here I was spouting philosophy and morality. It wasn't long before people started avoiding me.

"It was lonely in the beginning but I soon got used to it. And anyway, no one is ever really lonely in the city, provided their mind is switched on. The people that sleepwalk through their lives as if in a daydream, they are the ones who are truly lonely. They exist only to sustain myths and lies, filling their minds and bodies with useless crap. I don't subscribe to any of it—insurance, savings accounts, digital television, mobile phones, leather settees and foreign holidays. The leeches that run people's lives use that stuff to make them believe there's nothing else. I understand their deceptions better than they do, believe me!

"I got my freedom the day of the accident—no question about it—I'd still be driving about Paris blind to the world if it weren't for that accident. I mean, I still drive around Paris, but at least I know why I do it now—to bear witness to this great modern mess, to deconstruct or to confound it.... All the same, it was the accident that set me on the right path and I've been a long time waiting for another one— obviously the same accident can't happen again. It's just that I don't know sometimes if I'm wasting my time or not."

"Wouldn't the answer to that question be in one of Barthes' books?" I asked. "Yes, of course. If only I could decipher it. Perhaps he'd have shed more light on my dilemma, if I had left him more time. Perhaps his mind was on it as he lay in his hospital bed in Pitié-Salpêtrière, unable to breathe for himself such were the injuries he'd received in the accident. Perhaps that was their subject of conversation when he had dinner that very evening with Mitterand and Foucault. He was hurrying from them when he headed towards rue des Écoles—plenty of wine in his system and after a nice cigar, no doubt. He was hurrying to his mother's house, like the good and loyal son he always was. Perhaps he had the answer to some question that had been perplexing him, who knows. I always imagine there was a fresh breeze in his face and that he felt like he was walking up some heavenly corridor. I was hurrying as well—around the corner. I bent forward to light a cigarette and *bang*."

I pulled myself out of the café, lest it should fall into another time-trough. Outside, an emerald-coloured lorry was sweeping the litter from the side of the street with a couple of men following to pick up what it had missed. There was no way home now but to get the *noctambus*, an irregular service that collected the final stragglers from the streets before disappearing in a haze towards the end of the night.

Kango

It was the awful pounding at the end of the street that woke him from sleep. They had been drilling holes in the road down there for the previous four weeks—diggers and *kangos* initially, and now with that one mighty drill they called the pile-driver; like underground thunder, the constant mighty throb of it. He nearly tripped on the floor he was in such a hurry to get his shirt and trousers on, and the walls of the house convulsing with every smash of the mega drill. He didn't delay to tie his shoelaces as he hurried out of the bedroom. By the time he was at the back door the racket seemed to have eased a bit. His mother and father were sitting on a bench in the garden as they usually did this time of year drinking tea. They welcomed him to the day without overdoing it as they knew he could be cranky in the mornings and they wouldn't do anything that might make him leave and live somewhere else.

"Cup of tea?"

"No. Do you not hear those damn machines down there?"

"No", they answered, with a look of apology, but it was true. The pile-driver had stopped.

At the bottom of the street, he stopped for breath and looked into the hole they'd made. It was as deep as anything he'd ever seen with supports at the sides and smaller cavities leading off them at various points through the rock; and way down the bottom, the silty dark water radiating purple streaks in the light. He began to think of the caves under the *subway* in New York where hundreds of homeless people lived, apparently—a Dante's *Inferno* winding its way down in a series of warrens all the way to the filthy lair of the Devil himself. He had his own place reserved in that same Inferno, if the Italian professor who'd spent the best part of three months insulting him and shaming him into doing some other course was right; so much so that in the end he'd left college and gone working with a newspaper. He still remembered some of the verses he'd got bogged down in:

"One day, in the middle of the afternoon, I went looking for myself…"

"Stop, stop, stop."

"Vicky, could you save us from this blasphemy. I don't know what part of the Inferno we'll assign you to McCullough given your complete travesty of Dante's language."

"'In the middle of the journey of our life I found myself within a dark woods where the straight way was lost.'"

His mobile phone pulsed inside his shirt pocket and he saw his name flash up in capitals—Gibson.

"Hello. Yes. Yes. On my way."

Waiting for a bus. It's nearly here. Look! What else can I honestly tell you? It's not like anyone's going to shoot you for delaying the story slightly. My life's in danger because of all this. Listen, I'll be with you in a while."

It was easy to "play" Gibson, the editor—or "handle him" as the Special Branch would put it. All you had to do was let on that you were ready to explode with the enormity of the story—and he'd be phoning you twenty times a day—on the assumption that more pressure would help you get the story delivered. Everyone had their own ways and "patterns," some more complicated than others. And it was from his father and mother that he'd inherited his ability to read people and recognize how they operated. In fact, his parents still got the same wry amusement out of it all as he did—the ridiculous things that people got up to and the mess they found themselves in afterwards. Their way was the same as his. Let someone else do the talking, but just do enough to keep them talking all the same. Then, come evening, whenever the neighbours or visitors were gone, they'd go over each small titbit of news in detail again until their faces turned puce with that silent inner laughter of theirs. They'd have wrested secrets from the stones.

He, however, had brought this talent to a whole new level. The childish nuggets of gossip his parents heard from their neighbours were never enough for him. He always wanted something more. As soon as he left school, he decided to use his talent for gossip for his own benefit through his work as a journalist, enticing all sorts of stories and scandals from people and the newspaper-owners had made a whole heap of money out of it too. And even then he was still a bit too similar to his parents at times—like someone winding the handle of the machine every now and then—to keep the thing running. In theory, anyone could do this. What he really wanted was to follow the most interesting and convoluted patterns that underlay things, those undercurrents behind the churn of daily life. Once he did this, his gifts really began to blossom. He began prompting people to do things that they'd never have done if they hadn't been tipped off by him in the first place—other journalists, politicians, civil servants, special branch men and the like—and then he'd sit back and have a good laugh at the labyrinth of games and manoeuvrings he'd kicked off and all the shenanigans people got up to.

On one occasion when the police searched the house of a particular television broadcaster believing that they'd find drugs there he was ecstatic. As easy as that! He created so many similar situations by sending some people out to search for dirt on others, then having others watching their own backs for no reason and encouraging others again to break the law—and all the while he'd sit back watching the strange connections and twisted patterns he'd instigated, and laughing his head off at the whole thing. It was like a *flea circus* after a while. He was like someone who'd thousands of shares in thousands of companies and all he had to do was glance at the newspapers the odd time to make sure everything was running smoothly. He kept at it for a good while and, if nothing else, it helped ease the frustration of having to deal with some of his colleagues on a daily basis—especially Gibson. It was a hell of a lot easier to get through the day when you had this little parallel universe going on, one that he'd imagined for himself but which was nevertheless real—so real that it was physically dangerous. And the best thing of the lot was that he could manipulate the patterns he'd created and nurture them in his own time and at his own bidding, exactly as one might do with a work of art. Over time, however, these patterns and configurations of his became too obvious and so he decided on one big final project that would blow apart all the rest. He decided to create his own *alter ego*.

He set to work immediately selecting particular people that he could work on—subtly feeding them titbits of stories every now and then, and directing them—unknown to them—on how to join the dots together. He loved the sudden flash of recognition in their eyes when they realized the significance of the "major story" they were sitting on—and more incredibly still, their conviction that he—the king of all journalists—had been blind to it all along! This was how he created *Kango*. He built up his alter ego carefully over time until every Tom, Dick and Harry actually believed that it was true—there actually was someone out there directing this whole sorry mess of 30 years of conflict and one person was responsible for it all. Needless to say, Gibson wasn't long coming to him with the "big one," a story that would make their names forever.

"If you could nail this one for us," Gibson said, practically breathless with excitement, "if you could get us this one, every media and news outlet in the world would want it and we'd be set up for life."

"*We'd* be set up?"

"Absolutely. Just you and me! All you have to do now is get out there and nail it before someone else does."

The bomb was primed. But they had to bide their time for the big news corporations to get the scent and for everything to build momentum—like a great festering boil ready to burst. Next thing, the speculation and the blame game kicked off—anywhere where this *Kango* individual could possibly be embedded. *Kango* was someone incredibly well-connected who could manipulate every aspect of the media in accordance with their whims. I mean who would get up to something like this? What would they gain out of it? Only the antichrist himself would do something like this, a demon from the darkest depths of hell but then again—you never could tell. Weren't there doctors and nurses out there who'd regularly murdered their patients until they'd finally been nabbed? Weren't there even some twisted people in the world who put broken glass into baby-food products? There was no logic to such people, but they certainly existed—they were out there in the world and psychologists would tell you that, evil as they were, they couldn't help themselves.

"Cully, Cully, Cully…"

Gibson looked so happy he was in danger of kissing him.

"McCullough, my dear boy, you're finally here."

"The buses in this city are a mess, the same as everything else! I thought you'd never make it but look, we'll be sitting by the Med sipping wine before you know it! How long before we can release the story?"

His face was flushed and red—just like his parents.

"Well, seeing as you've the money transferred, there's no reason why I can't be gone within the next day or two."

"Yes, but what about the story?"

"I'll zap it onto you straight away as soon as I'm out of here. I have to watch out."

"Yes, of course. But if you go down, you're going to bring a few other people down with you, aren't you?

23

Isn't that what you're supposed to say at a moment like this?"

"Exactly."

Coming out of the newspaper office's main reception, he pulled his flight details from his pocket—16 hours to go.

He had to pass the remaining hours somehow but there was no way he could go back to his parent's place. What would he say to them anyway? Or were they so intuitive that they already knew what he'd done? He hung around town until it got dark and got the last bus up the road.

It was only manners to let them know something of what he'd planned, to give them some small hint of how their lives were going to change. And who knows? Maybe, they'd actually be proud of how he'd used their great talent—the great coup he'd just pulled off. But when he got off the bus he went no further than the giant hole at the end of the street. All he could make out was the black pool of water at the bottom, silent as the grave. The gaping hole was surrounded by great metal bars so that no-one would fall in, either that or there was some wild animal in there resting quietly in the darkness.

He stood there momentarily and then turned on his heels. It was all sorted, Gibson would get the story tomorrow.

"Gibson, my dear boy, *you* are *Kango.*"

The Drama Group

There were just three songs left. *Frosty the Snowman, Chestnuts Roasting on an Open Fire, O Little Town of Bethlehem*. Once that tape was finished she'd go out and bring in the two Christmas trees, then switch off the lights. She walked up through the shop throwing a reluctant glance at the Christmas baubles to make sure they were all in the right place. Some of the office crowd were already passing the front window and she could hear the lad selling newspapers down at the corner. She turned and went over to the phone waiting on the call from Tony, the manager. "Angela. Closing time. Many in today? Ah well. Never mind. Bye."

It was ten years ago now that Tony had first employed her in the Christmas shop and it was like living in a doll's house at that time of the year. Tony was a flighty sort of a fellow and he thought that it'd be nice to have a shop selling Christmas stuff all-year around. He wasn't too bothered about making a profit. It was the principle of the thing. He felt that the city needed a place like this and she was happy to row in on it and support him.

She hunkered down to put the padlock on the metal grid. The path outside was like a furnace with pieces of chewing gum encrusted with dirt slowly melting in the heat. A gentle breeze raised her hair just as a tall young woman whizzed by on skates. She turned around and watched her nylon-clad backside weave a path through the crowd until she gradually disappeared from sight. There was some kind of a ruckus down at the corner of the street and people were moving in to the side and looking behind them at whatever it was. Before she knew what was going on, a young lad was standing one side of her and another lad on the other, both trying to hit each other with bags of water. For a second, she stared into his eyes pleading with him not to throw it at her but it was no good. The water-balloon burst right next to her and soaked her hair—and left all down her left-hand side, drowned-wet. Without so much as a glance behind her, she disappeared quickly down the road and left the raucous laughter of that crowd of morons behind her. There was a time once when she'd have made some effort to fight back against that cheeky little brat, and given him a mouthful of abuse—at the very least—but what was the point? These days, she preferred just to ignore them. It could happen to anyone and it wasn't as if they were out to get her more than anyone else. It wasn't easy. But this was how it was in a city like this—the biggest morons had the run of the place. The ones with the least imagination, the least feeling. It wasn't just the people of course. The buildings had no feeling, the streets lacked all character and the shops were dead. True to form, people had had a good laugh when the Christmas shop first opened in the middle of summer.

She thought back to the time when she'd worn the *bandana* a friend had brought back for her from South America as a present. She was a student back then and it was fine to wear it in the area around the University but when she was going home on the bus one afternoon a bunch of schoolboys had started mocking her. The sniggering and derision had started the minute she reached the top of the stairs and as soon as she sat down it was shouts of Rambo! Stallone! Wonder Woman! They burst out laughing every time but the biggest laugh of all was when she turned around to them and it was clear that she was in a temper. They really got going then. The shouting and roaring and laughter carried right down the length of the bus. She got into a fit of coughing which kicked the whole thing off again.

At least now she didn't have to get the bus. Ten minutes and she'd be up in the University quarter, far from the town dullards. She wasn't alone in this. Hadn't Sartre referred to Le Havre as *Boueville*? Bally-muck is what she'd have called this place if she ever wrote anything about it. Her type needed something

27

like this, a place free of stupidity and moronic behaviour—a place with more bicycles *per capita* than anywhere else, a place where people drank coffee instead of tea, and where posters decorated the walls willing people to join various revolutionary organizations. It was no Greenwich Village but at least she felt it wasn't the struggle it was in other places. Little things gave her respite—the way the red-brick buildings looked noble in evening sunshine. Or the sight of the moon whenever she was crossing the railway bridge at night—like a spirit that'd come out for her alone. It was easier to put up with the other stuff when you had these small moments of wonder.

She gave a little smile as she viewed the length of her street from the corner, the bosom of every house-front proudly raised to the day—like the women back in the days when those houses were first built. She noticed that leaflets had been stuck into the letterbox of every house except her own. Either that or someone had swiped one from hers. She slowed down for a second as a blue pall of smoke wound its way slowly above the hedge, dizzy in the sunlight.

"Well, Angela. Where's the party on?"

"Dessie. Christ," I didn't know who was standing there! Are you pissed?"

"No" he said, jamming a pack of *rizla* into his pocket.

"How long are you there?"

"What? In the country or in the street here? You've done something with your hair. It looks nice."

He stood back so that she could get her key in the door, then followed her inside."

"Potpourri?"

"Patchouli."

"Sorry, I never did *aromatherapy* at school."

"That's easy to tell."

"Well, you wouldn't smell great either if you were off travelling as long as me…"

She fell back in the armchair and stretched out her two legs. Dessie plonked himself on the couch and began to scratch his stubbly face.

"Aren't you going to give me an ashtray?"

"You know I don't smoke. When did you start yourself? This must be the only vice you hadn't picked up—until now that is.

"I was working for a crowd who were promoting smoking. They let on that they were just a normal company, people concerned about civil liberties but the tobacco companies were behind them of course. They used to give out cigarettes free of charge and you were kind of under pressure to smoke if you were working there. Their name was 'Freedom to Use and Consume Tobacco'."

"'FUCT'."

"Exactly."

She gave him a stare, looked him up and down.

"Christ, what has become of the revolution?"

"It could be worse. I could be working in a shop that sells Christmas goods from one end of the year to the next. Anyway, I got some radio work recently and someone is to come back to me about a few different parts—television dramas—I'm not talking soaps here."

"Don't forget who gave you your first part and who brought you into the drama society the first day ever."

"Well, you saw the talent in me I suppose and, of course, I was really into you."

"A hard look came into her eyes then as much as to say that he had insulted her."

"Do you mind me asking? What are you doing here, so?"

"I'm just here for a couple nights, a bit longer if you'll let me."

"I don't think you get it. Those days are gone now Dessie—the days when people can just drop in whenever they feel like it—en route to somewhere else, somewhere better usually. This isn't a place for people to stop off in on the way to California any more. You'd swear sometimes that people deliberately called in here so that they could savour wherever they were really headed all the more.

"Do you not hear from the others anymore?"

"I do—if you call the odd postcard hearing from them—or a phone call once in a blue moon. I'm like an old granny and everyone belonging to her gone away."

Well, you were always a bit of a mammy in fairness. Always minding the rest of us like."

"Yeah. Not like you Dessie."

She went out to the kitchen and put on the kettle. She took a few pills from a box in the press and swallowed them, then shouted into him. "I've nothing in. But I did I made a big pot of *shoko* last night— enough to feed an entire family. Will you have some?"

"Sure. Whatever's going Angela, whatever it is, I'll have it."

"It's a kind of a stew. From Africa. It's not easy to get ingredients in this city to make nice food. Too many ignoramuses around the place. They all get their food at Tesco and their clothes down at JJB Sports and that's it. But *shoko* is easy enough to make though."

She brought in two bowls of it and a few slices of bread.

"Thanks very much and *bon appetit*. Or whatever they say over in Africa."

"I don't remember anymore."

They ate in silence for a moment.

"This place here. It's kind of an *oasis* in the desert, Angela."

"How do you mean?"

"Well, y'know, with your patchouli and *shoko* and all that.

But that was always you—in fairness. Sure, wasn't it you who started the living statues before anyone else had ever even heard of it?"

"Yeah, that was me, all right. I started everything in this place but what did I get for my troubles? Friends?"

"Ah, I don't know. What does anyone get out of it? People like us. People who don't care about money, we have to get our satisfaction from other things."

They fell quiet again and Angela was the first to speak.

"So, what makes you happy these days?"

"I haven't a bean and I just live from day to day. There's a certain satisfaction in that, I suppose. And I've got a *gig* in the student's union tomorrow night. That'll be a bit of crack."

"A gig?"

"Yeah, I'm doing DJ."

"Worse than I thought. Have you nothing else you could be doing—instead of playing tunes?"

"There's a certain pleasure comes with it, like the buzz you get from acting. You'd have to be there to understand. And sure, we all have to do something to pass the time, don't we? I mean—what can you do? It's easy enough to come into the world and leave it again but what we do in between? That's the question, isn't it?"

That hard look had returned to Angela's eyes.

"Not everyone finds it easy to 'leave the world', as you put it, Dessie."

"How do you mean?"

"You know well what I mean."

"Hang on. What are you saying?"

She brought the empty bowls out to the kitchen. On her return, he stared at her as much as to say that he was still waiting for an explanation.

"What do you mean Angela?" he said eventually. She got up and opened one of the windows, giving it a rough tug. She couldn't look him in the face this time.

"That's another thing about the old crowd. They're great for remembering the old friends who aren't around anymore, aren't they?"

"Sorcha, you mean?"

"Exactly Dessie. Good man yourself."

"Weren't you with her the night she died?"

I was. We all were."

"I wasn't," Angela said.

"What difference does that make?"

"If I'd been there that night, she might have had a chance. If she'd had someone there to keep an eye on her. I brought her into the group and the rest of you ended up killing her."

"What do you mean 'the rest of you'?"

"Exactly that. The rest of you? Where are you all now? Who were you lot to destroy someone anyway?"

"Hang on. She killed herself. Everyone knows that," Dessie said, giving her an incredulous stare.

"Is this how you talk to someone who calls in for a visit these days? Is this how you get rid of them? Sitting there accusing your friends of responsibility for someone else's death. Jesus! Of course you're Miss Perfect, aren't you? The Queen of the Theatre, now resident in *Lapland* if you don't mind! There was never anyone as arty or creative as you either, was there? There was nobody quite good enough for you!"

Angela got up and walked over to the phone.

"Yeah, there you go. Call the police, why don't you. Tell them you've some big-time murderer in the house with you, why don't you?"

"I'm calling a taxi for you right now," Angela seethed.

Neither of them said anything.

The sounds of the street outside grew louder. Students drinking and chatting noisily. A group of girls passed the house, the click-clack of their shoes on the path outside.

Dessie smiled:

"Angela. Come with me to the gig tomorrow night and it will be your salvation. You don't have to do anything—just watch the gig, that's all. We'll be on-stage the two of us, looking down at the crowd. All they'll see is a few shadows moving behind the lights. They'll pay us no attention but all the time, it will be our music driving them on. You've never seen the like of it. Five hundred people dancing as one in a great sea of joy and every single one of them right there in the palm of our hands. You could never get enough of it. And if that doesn't heal you, then nothing will."

Angela leaned back in her chair. The noise on the street out front grew louder. They listened in silence, imagining the night just beginning. She only barely heard the sound of the taxi outside, then muttered drowsily to Dessie,

"Just ignore him. He'll leave again in a minute."

The False Gods
St Brendan's College, 1986

"It appears they had a black mass in Paris," said the Canon.

"And was anyone sacrificed at all? A virgin maybe, or a goat?" asked Roche.

"No. They had to make do without any sacrificial victim, by all accounts."

"Such a pity the Devil wasn't paid his dues. Was Mitchell in the Moulin Rouge while this was going on or was it him who found Morgan reading this "mass" of theirs?"

"I was in the *Moulin Rouge* myself back when it was worth being there, right at the end of the war, forty years ago," answered the Canon, "but here, the other two are coming now. I'll tell them to bring in the tea."

Once all four had gathered together, the Canon asked them to sit down and the meeting began.

"Gentlemen. We're here to discuss the case of Pearse Morgan and to determine if he has a future here with us at all. He's been giving trouble for some time now and after all this carry on in Paris, he'll either be suspended or expelled from the college and we'll be rid of him altogether.

"One way or another, we'll be placing obstacles before him on the great road of life," said Fr. Murphy.

"Yes Father, the same as *Odysseus* who was lost at sea while the gods decided his fate."

"*Odysseus?*" queried Roche—"Morgan created these obstacles for himself, as we all know."

"Whatever decision we make here now," rasped the Canon from the back of his throat, "we mustn't forget that we've a responsibility towards more than one boy."

"And that we're educating men for the society of the future. The Jesuits have a saying…"

"They say more than their prayers," said the Canon, interrupting Roche again.

"What I want at this meeting," he continued, "is to gather evidence and information so that I can make a decision in this fellow's case. Maybe Mr Mitchell can tell us what was done in the name of Beelzebub in Paris and I'm not referring to the places of ill-repute that you frequent yourself on these trips, master."

"Well Canon, we had no trouble whatsoever until the very last night. They were given the afternoon off to buy presents before leaving, and when I checked their bags, I found nothing worse than some of the *bangers* that they've been setting off in the quadrangle ever since. But like I say, I didn't come across anything that was immoral or illegal. That's what made me think it'd be worth giving their rooms a quick raid in case something untoward was afoot."

"And tell us what untoward business you discovered then?"

"They were engaged in black magic, candles lit on a table complete with grotesque-looking symbols and that little skitter Morgan right in the middle of it all, running the show. Needless to say, I grabbed him by the throat the minute I realized what they were up to but he made no excuses for it, nor did he try to blame any of the others either."

"Seeing as he wouldn't have a leg to stand on, if he did! Reverend Fathers and fellow-colleagues," proclaimed Roche, "we have enough evidence here to expel the little heretic and be rid of him for good."

Father Murphy jammed his finger under his collar and loosened it in an effort to let the air in.

"Can any of you explain to me what crime this boy has committed?"

"I don't know what kind of mass you used to say in El Salvador, Father, but we don't go in for this form of worship over here," Roche remonstrated, straightening himself in his chair.

The Canon gave a dismissive chuckle: "This wasn't a black mass from what I'm hearing. It was just some kind of séance where they were messing around with a Ouija board. Now I don't know what kind of neurosis this young lad suffers from but what I do know is that his father died when he was still in the junior school. Maybe he thought he could call on the "spirit" of his dead father if he got this board to work or something? Some sort of stupidity like that—that's what they were at, I'd say. But that's of no importance to us. While we may *understand* things up here that doesn't mean we can excuse them down there. He walked over to the window and looked out onto the quadrangle below.

But Roche began again:

"I really don't care what happens to this little weasel's soul to be honest, but for the sake of the college, I recommend that we expel him—throw him out on the street and he can educate himself after that.

"Yes. Let's expel him," says Mitchell.

"And what about you Father?" asked the Canon, turning back from the window.

"You know, maybe the decision's already made and he *is* better off being thrown out into the big world right now," Father Murphy replied.

So, we're all agreed then that..?

Father Murphy interrupted Roche as though he hadn't heard him at all.

"I'm sitting here in this fine oak chair, "looking at this silver dish in the middle of the table and the artificial fruit in it and I'm wondering whether I travelled five thousand miles from South America for this. Maybe, when I first went out there, I was a bit innocent, maybe I thought I was going to bring some of this wealth to the poverty-stricken masses living in the wretched little huts of El Salvador. I know now that it was they who passed on the faith to me and it was they who made me realize that I should become a missionary over here instead. That said, I'm afraid I'm not sure where to begin—or how to explain that country in a place like this."

"I can't see what that has to do with the case we're discussing here," mumbled Roche, as he glanced impatiently in the direction of the Canon.

Father Murphy turned to him.

"The way it relates to this lad's situation and all the other lads in this institution here is that we're suffocating them with hypocrisy. There are lads here who lose interest in this college once they realize that there's no point in accumulating knowledge while the bigger picture remains unexplained. Maybe this young lad Morgan would be better-off educating himself as you say—but then again, he's already doing that as it is without anyone's permission."

"I suppose that's what you were at in your classes over there Father, was it—teaching them the "bigger picture?" Roche looked intently at the Canon all the while, as though abandoned by him.

Later, when Roche and the Canon were finally alone he noticed a slight flush in the principal's cheeks. He wouldn't dare reproach the Canon for not putting "Father Guevara" in his place but it angered him more than ever that this old goat had all the authority while the likes of himself was breaking his arse trying to keep the place going. Still and all—you had to play the game.

"In fairness Canon, I don't know what the point is of the rest of us listening to Father Murphy's rambling opinions when we've serious decisions to make."

There was a sharpness to the Canon's words this time however, as if he'd been riled somehow. Roche rarely saw him like this but he recognized the signs straight away—the pursing of the lips and the half-whistling sound as he spoke.

"I've spent my entire life in this college from when I was first sent here at the age of twelve. And if I'm the master of anything, I'm the master of these walls and what lies within them—that is the definition of an institution, Roche. Father Murphy doesn't belong to this world. The likes of him come and go and do nothing but keep the bishops busy, and maybe we should be grateful to them for that doing that much. As regards this fellow Morgan, a letter will be sent out to his mother this afternoon and he'll never again set foot inside the front gate of this College.

A certain light reappeared in the Canon's eyes. "But weren't we talking about the Moulin Rouge there a while ago?" he says.

Anyway, I was dragged along to this place one night—the young innocent chaplain that I was—it must have been forty years ago now, the end of the war…"

Apparition

In through the big rubber doors we went, the same great whoosh from them as we got from the ghost train in Portrush years ago. The one that made your buttocks tighten as you grabbed the bar tight. Whatever about me, the two that were bringing me in on the trolley were more concerned than I was—both of them glancing anxiously down at the puddle of blood around my stomach. A swarm of nurses descended on us immediately, swearing and nearly falling on top of me in their haste. We sped up the corridors towards one of the rooms but all I could make out was the sight of the two builders on trolleys next to me, their faces streaked with blood and red-brick dust.

Then the dreams started. You'll understand them better than me, maybe.

There I was driving a *vespa* around Manhattan and the streets blocked off. I stopped and looked down 21st Street where an IRA funeral wound its way slowly between two skyscrapers. A while later, and I was in one of those old German films that you always made me watch—*Die Strasse*, it might have been. The streets were getting so dark that I couldn't make out anything. In the end, I found myself in a bed with some *Nosferatu* fellow bending over me sinking his giant fingernails into my chest. Whenever I woke up I knew I'd have been safer in the nightmare than in that hospital. I couldn't make out why I'd been brought there either, when there was a hospital in our own area that was safe. Rosa couldn't visit me here and I'd be lucky if I wasn't attacked again here too. Maybe they had no choice.

What had made me come home anyway? I'd no sooner arrived in the airport than the car was sprayed with a barrage of machine-gun fire. They must have thought that they'd hit her as they drove off up the road roaring out the windows that they'd killed that Republican bitch. But it was Rosa herself who got me into the ambulance and kept a tight hold of my hand—even if she couldn't go all the journey with me, needless to say.

They could never kill Rosa—nor injure her even—that was always the way. They should have realized that by now. She's always had this ability to be in the right place at the right time and you can't reproach her for that—it's just in her nature. I stopped being jealous of her years ago—even before I went to New York first. There was no point. I wasn't on her level and that was it. As a child it had always annoyed me that she was always right, that and the way everything was directed at her instead of me—the boy. Then when I was around seventeen, the gap between us grew even wider. She had her own life going on and her own friends. I'd notice the big lads from the final year in school staring at me. I think that they were surprised that an unremarkable little wretch like me could be related to "Granuaile". But they weren't in the same league as her either. She'd wouldn't look at the same side of the street as boys her own age. She left them for dead, as she did me. There was just no stopping her. She'd only have passed one milestone when she'd be onto the next. Stories did the rounds about two who were high up in "the movement" that had pulled guns on each other one night on account of her. And her spying exploits were inscribed in legend. My aunt thought all that stuff had come to an end when she announced one day that she was leaving for North Africa on a university fellowship. There was no talk in those days of the movement's 'international links', needless to say. I sensed that I was better off moving on myself then too. It's not that I was running away or that I was afraid. I had been planning on emigrating for a long time because I couldn't get anywhere in that city the way things were. But what madness made me return?

I haven't had any visitors since I came in here and I can't get in touch with you wherever you are. Then sometime this morning this man arrives in that I haven't seen since I was at school. I woke up to find him standing there at the foot of the bed like he was addressing a crowd of children in class. Ringo—I had a job trying to remember his real name—Jack Starkey, the history teacher we'd had years ago. He still had the same bald head and the greasy comb-over and he was wearing one of those old blue raincoats from the Sixties. He was no Leonard Cohen though, I can tell you that much. He had always reminded me of someone who'd butchered loads of people but had managed to keep it under wraps from the rest of the world, like one of those old Nazis who'd created a new identity after the war. His face was fatigued and his eyes seemed exhausted as though from waiting. He woke me up from a deep sleep:

"For God's sake, you're not going to lie there all day like an old woman are you? Don't tell me you're beginning to get fond of the hospital food here?" He grabbed a hold of the bar at the end of the bed and roared with laughter.

"You wouldn't ever find me in one of these beds. This is where the weakest people are left to rot along with the rest of the wasters."

I propped myself up on one of my elbows.

"So where would *you* go Ringo if someone pumped your chest with a load of bullets? The staff room, I suppose?"

"You needn't be using nicknames with me sonny. That's a right you'll never have. What's this about your ribs being pumped full of lead? Living in fantasy-

46

land again as usual? Staring out the window like the bloody fool you always were?"

"If you're talking about the years I spent in your class, I wouldn't have been asleep in the first place if you'd had anything interesting worth saying."

"Oh! Well, excuse me sir for wasting your precious time!

I suppose that you were educated since in some fancy college abroad somewhere. Somewhere with eminent professors who could satisfy your thirst for knowledge seeing as you wouldn't dream of bothering with all that stupid, dull stuff I used to try and force into that tiny brain of yours: you know—the truth, basic facts, wretched though you find them ?"

"Yes, I managed to get an education despite you in the end... what are you doing here anyway? Is your life so empty now that you've to go around annoying former pupils? I suppose you saw a report about the attack on television.... well, you can leave the fruit at the end of the bed and piss off."

"What attack are you on about, young lad? Bullets you say? Were there many of them in the spaceship? Did they have antennae on them—pointing out of their backsides?"

I tried to raise myself in the bed and grab him by the neck but I couldn't move. There was no feeling at all in my legs. I was his prisoner. He started to question me again—circling the bed with a swagger now that he knew I couldn't get near him. I tried to ignore him, to put him out of my mind by pretending he wasn't there but he just wouldn't leave.

"When were you shot? How many times? Where were you hurt? Nothing to say for yourself?"

Shame on you for lying through your teeth like this! Answer me, why don't you! When I was at school, the master would give you plenty of leather if you didn't answer him straight away! I was always way too easy on you, that was my problem!"

"I was shot three times in the ribs you gobshite!"

"Show me so!"

I don't know why I even bothered but I tried pointing at where I was hit.

"Nothing?"

"More lies again. I was afraid it'd be like this. After all your talk it was just nonsense. Acting as though you were our Lord showing his wounds to Thomas."

"For my own sanity, Ringo, I'm not going to respond to that one. I came in on a flight from New York, where I live, last night. My sister picked me up at the airport and her car was ambushed. They've been trying to kill her for years. I was brought here by ambulance drenched in blood with some bullets, that weren't there previously, in my ribs."

"New York, you say! Well, good for you!"

"What do you do over there—if you don't mind me asking?"

"I'm an architect."

"Oh, of course you are!"

"Married with kids?"

"I have a partner. She's a lecturer in Film Studies."

"That's why I was dreaming earlier. She's always got old films and foreign films on in the flat."

"What university is she in?"

"Columbia."

"Columbia! Where else, in God's name!"

"And where is she now, this woman of yours and where is your famous sister as well?"

"You'd think that a woman who's a lecturer in Colombia would be on the first plane from New York to be at your side, wouldn't you—especially seeing as you've been shot! It'd be like being in your own film!"

He was quiet for a moment and then launched into it again:

"Tell the truth. There's no such woman really, is there?

You made that up the same as everything else you've told me because you're one of those pathetic imbeciles who never amount to anything unless, of course, there's a living to be made from day-dreaming and scratching your backside!"

Whether out of exhaustion or despair, I was left with no reply. I focussed on the ceiling instead in the hope that he'd go away, but I was too interested in him. I spoke to him calmly and without a trace of anger in my voice:

"Why did you come in here to torment me anyway?"

"You know well why I'm here. Don't think that I came here off my own bat. You sent for me."

I waited for an explanation.

"Truth is, you called on the only trustworthy source you have left in that head of yours—me. You asked yourself 'what do I know?' And you found the answer in me."

"Now—here's the question. What do you know?"

I shut my eyes and tried to shift to somewhere else in my mind. A shadow engulfed the room and all I could see was his shape between me and the light, his two hands fixed to the bottom of the bed, leaning down over me. He never moved but I could feel him staring at me in the half-light of the room. Whenever I glanced up he was still standing there, his bulk like a dark pillar, his breath laboured and slow.

The Hermit

"Where's the cigarette machine?" he asked one day in a hotel. When he was told where the machine was he made his way across the hotel floor with the same heavy, unwavering steps of his, clumps of muck falling from his boots onto the carpet as he went. His face looked no different. The red patches on his face and the broken veins above the cheeks as before. It was just that his face was moist like the walls of a house that was rotting with damp. He lit a cigarette at the bar and ordered a pint of lager. He gave a grunt when the pint arrived, and began to flick the bottom of the cigarette against his thumb. This was his first time in this hotel and he wouldn't be back either. £2.50 for a pint of bog-water. By Christ, but these people had it easy... but there was no use in talking. He gave a quiet laugh to himself—he was never good at talk. He preferred to be in the little shed he'd built for himself at the back of the house. He had everything he needed there—every tool and knickknack under the sun—stuff that even mechanics and fitters wouldn't have known of. The wonders of the world lay in that shed.

The "talk" with herself came back to him again now. It was like something physical—a piece of tough meat that he hadn't digested. "I wouldn't like to bring children into the world with you for a father." Well, there was no fear of that anyway. Wasn't she as barren as the desert itself, and the whole world knew it.

She'd never have children. The doctors in the hospital had told her this often enough. But whatever it was about her—twenty doctors could have come over from *Harley Street* and told her the same thing— she wouldn't listen. Either that, or she'd pretend she'd got it until they were gone and then start on him again with the: "Y'know I'm not sure about what those doctors said. Some of them are only just out of college. You wouldn't want to be relying on them."

Well, the marriage was over now for sure. They wouldn't need any doctors to tell them that much. Pity he'd ever let them entice him into that whole spider's web the first day ever. Herself and her sister, the idiots. The sister, especially. He'd leased the shop to them after their last place closed down. His rent wasn't much seeing as the place was in a bit of a state. And yet, after all that, they hadn't made a success of the shop at all. They didn't seem to get it that sewing shops were a thing of the past—another one of those silly ideas they'd picked up from their mother. But whatever about that, you had to say that the sister had played the game well. That intense look she'd always give him, as much as to say that there was some important business between them that her sister wouldn't understand.

He didn't really care, in truth. He just found the whole thing sort of funny—the sister staring at him when he'd come into the shop, her chest puffed out like a peacock and her thinking all the while that this was the way she would get a foothold in his business—marry her excuse of a sister off on him and she'd be landed. And she'd been right, of course.

A small-set drunk stumbled across the floor bumping into him by accident. If the drunkard excused himself once, he must have excused himself twenty times, his face inches from his, all the while. The man's forehead furrowed in deep trenches as he strained to keep his big, watery eyes open at all. He gave the same sarcastic laugh to himself that he always gave on occasions like this. The world was full of little fools like this one. And he was an expert on fools. God knows, he'd spent enough time around them.

He had noticed how she'd become more like the sister as she settled into married life. The dark hair pulled back to the crown of her head, so tightly that the skin of her forehead was pink to the roots. He'd watch her every morning gripping the mass of oily hair in her fist to tie it back. She'd give it an almighty wrench on those mornings when she had the appointments with the doctors. But she'd never get any good news from them.

It was then that she'd gotten into all that nonsense, the priests being the start of it. Before then, the clergy had never bothered him much except to ask for money for some silly project or other. But they weren't long in leaving him alone for they were uncomfortable in his company. They knew that he had them well figured out for a bunch of bloodsuckers. Besides that, they were too posh for him. They'd sit down for a minute and look around in horror at the furniture and the pictures on the walls, trying all the while to contain their disgust. She'd started inviting the priests around once she'd given up on the doctors. And they'd visited a few times to gawp in amazement, probably, at this horrid couple— the man who'd only the torments of hell to look forward to, and the woman who was forever asking them questions regarding God's bounty and grace.

She kept at that for a while before she started going to the convent to pester the nuns. But by then she would listen to no one but herself and so the nuns were little help to her. And, of course, she did no work at all in the shop during all that time. The place was in her sister's hand alone at this stage and there wasn't a penny of rent out of her. In the end, he'd had to get rid of her and she cursed and damned him to hell like an old crow, as she left. The other one's only thought was for whatever the latest crowd of scoundrels was she was chasing after. And there was always plenty of scoundrels.

She'd arrived in one night after meeting a fortune-teller and started rambling on about the tree of life and a load of other things that made no sense. But she certainly didn't get her money's worth for there was only a few things here and there that came true—stuff about colours and numbers. The biggest thing she said was that she'd have a family and of course nothing at all came of that. From them on she was in thrall to these chancers. How ever much she'd hear from one of them, she'd have to see the next one—to get confirmation of what the first one had predicted. And when nothing tallied, she'd be told that every fortune-teller has their own vision of the future and every reading has its own truth.

Whatever she was told during all that time, she had great hopes for what the *Tarot* cards had said. There were five cards and the wand and the suit of cups on three of them. But the two she always got were "Death" and "The Hermit." The "Death" card was a long, twisted, skeleton, the "grim reaper" laying waste to everything before it with the scythe. She was told that her life would see a great change—a great transformation—the family she craved—and that it would happen very soon as well. A monk was pictured on the other card, "The Hermit", with a lamp in his hand as if guiding someone on their path. The reading for that card explained that her husband had his own strange ways all right—the way he spent all his days in that shed by himself—but that he was guiding her along all the while unknown to her. That much was true.

He drained back the last drop of his lager and put on his coat again. The waiter glanced anxiously at him when he noticed the trail of muck he'd left behind on their nice red carpet—not that he cared. Out on the street again, he noticed that it'd been raining for the afternoon and a dark, starry sky was over the town. That last conversation kept returning to his mind despite his best efforts—"I wouldn't like to bring children into the world with you for a father." It was when she'd called him a tramp that he had turned and gone back into her. It was a word he didn't care for.

After a short while he had arrived at the hill above the street, looking down at the row of houses all lit-up, his own little place included. But on this occasion there was a small crowd of people at the front of the house and the back garden was a blaze of light. There was a large white tent around the shed and the people that he could make out were also wearing white. And that was where herself and her sister were, curled up beneath the floorboards.

Talking to the Dead

I was working on a big book at that time, one about about ghosts and other "supernatural phenomena," one that would have pictures on bright glossy paper and a striking cover designed by an artist. I'd started out thinking about a book that I'd read when I was working as a photographer in the city centre. A woman who worked as a cleaner had given me a loan of it one day and said that it would shake me to the soles of my boots. It wasn't your usual thing about some spooky old roadhouse out in the remote countryside. This book was an account of things that happened in a Belfast housing estate. It described places that I was familiar with and people that I knew to see. One of them was Father Vincent who lived in the monastery. He was the diocesan exorcist apparently, something that I hadn't known until I read the book. I thought it best to start with him, interview him first and then take a black-and-white photo of him in the monastery, something really Gothic, the camera peering down at him from a height in his big black soutane at the door of the monastery, looking like Saint Michael the Archangel.

I arranged to meet him a couple times but he had to cancel every time. Then, by chance one day, I spotted a headline in the morning paper—"Exorcist's Death a Great Loss". He was dead! Christ—what a time to die! I began to make other plans. I'd get a photo of the priest in the coffin and the rosary beads wrapped around his fingers, I thought to myself. The exorcist and his paraphernalia on their way to the next world as it were—like an elderly chieftain. However, when I asked permission from the monastery to take such a photo, they refused. I thought of sneaking into the monastery at night when no one was looking and grabbing a quick photo that way—but the monastery had granted me permission to examine Father Vincent's papers. I was afraid that I'd lose this chance if I was caught taking the photo on the sly. As it turned out, there wasn't anything much in his papers. Just a load of stuff about sea-birds because the priest had been a leading member of an ornithological society and had spent his whole life gathering pictures and magazines about varieties of these birds. I came across the odd phone number and scrap of paper relating to his exorcist responsibilities but nothing useful. I decided to go looking for a copy of the book the cleaner had loaned me previously.

I knew it was out of print but I had the name and the address of the publisher—some place up on the

Antrim Road. I had no trouble finding it, a big ram-shackle building of an ugly colour—bicycle-green, a colour I have always hated. But when I went in I was given a great welcome. A young woman was the only person in the place and I could tell that I was the only one to call in that day, even if it was already after 4 o'clock in the afternoon. She offered me a cup of tea and chatted to me a mile to a minute—like someone who hadn't seen anyone for days. Not only did she give me a copy of the book she gave me five extra copies and another book on a different subject as well. She explained that the place was closing down before long and they had to get rid of any extra stock they had left. I thanked her and left her there on the top story of the building with a sad Rapunzel-like look in her eyes.

I spent that night reading the book and I felt the same horror surge up through me again just the same as the first time I'd read it. There was something in it for sure, no doubt about it. Every night after that I lay awake not out of terror but overcome instead by wonder and astonishment. Whatever way that book affected me, I couldn't think about anything except ghosts—those spirits that surround us each moment of the day watching us, and even laughing at us. If such things really existed, then we'd all have to look at everything again. And if that were true then many other things could be true also—God, of course, and transubstantiation, the fairies, Santa Claus. Everything that I'd rejected while growing up might have always have been true. How would you deal with such a transformation? I appreciated what people must go through who find out as adults that they've always had a twin whom they've never known—other than in the womb. The way they have to go back to the very beginning and get to know their own flesh-and-blood all over again. Perhaps the challenge would be too great, perhaps it would have been better never to have made such a discovery at all. It reminded me of a programme one night on television about a man who'd spent ten years doing research on the devil. Afterwards, he'd said that he'd never recommend it to anyone else given how much he'd begun to question his own lack of belief. I felt there was something unhealthy about the way my mind had become obsessed by this project, living off death and the dead, trying to prove that there was something there after all.

Once I'd gathered as much research on the subject as I could, I decided to take a break from it. I didn't look at anything to do with the project for the next three months and felt that this would be enough time to help clear my mind. It wasn't easy though and despite my best efforts, I was still as obsessed with the project a few months later. And yet, I felt that I still didn't have enough material to do justice to my enthusiasm for *The Great Book of the Dead*—as I'd provisionally titled my book.

Just I was beginning to despair, I came across something that I'd been waiting on for a long time. I was lying on the couch one night watching television—I'd lost all interest in newspapers and books at this stage—even if I'd always been suspicious of people who spend their whole lives in front of television sets, in case they might miss something important. But there I was that night, doing just that, except that what I saw was like a visitation from the Holy Spirit. I jumped up off the couch to find the remote so that I could record it. I was so excited that I tossed the remote aside as quickly again however—afraid that I'd miss even a second of what was on.

A special guest appeared on a late-night talk-show, a man who claimed that he could talk to the dead. Not only that, but the dead were passing him on information about various people who were in the studio audience:

"There's a woman here who wants to say something to John. She says that he shouldn't be worried about the child, that the boy's with her there and that he's very happy." A man in the audience bowed his head and tried to hold back the tears. Then there were other messages from various dead people that weren't half as serious as the first one. "Nora. Alison says that you should go to a different hairdresser."

It went on like this for about twenty minutes and when the ads came on, I got up and paced around the room. I went over everything I'd just seen in my mind until all that was left was the image of your man, talking to the dead. There was something strange about him, a lack of symmetry, with his one watery, bulging eye and the other dry and withered, one side of his face chubby and red, and the other emaciated and thin. He kept his chair at an angle for the duration of the television programme so that you couldn't see the withered side of him but it was clear that one half of his body was the opposite of the other—as if he'd had a twin who'd been separated from one side of his body.

I called into the television station the next day to try and get the man's phone number or get in touch with him somehow. The receptionist told me that other people had arrived in ahead of me enquiring about the same man. Apparently, he held sessions in various hotels around the country where he communicated with the dead. He produced a brochure from behind the counter which gave details including the man's contact information. "A Night in the company of Lesley Ormonde" was printed in bold letters across the top. I phoned the number and got through to him straight away. He was in Dublin preparing for a series of "nights" he was holding there. Sure. He could meet up with me any time that suited. He suggested we meet up one afternoon in a pub close to Christchurch Cathedral for a short while. I spent the day of our meeting wandering around various art galleries and museums in Dublin city centre. I found it difficult to focus my attention on any one thing or stay in any one place. It was like putting in the time before taking a flight home from somewhere abroad, oblivious to everything around you in the knowledge that you are leaving everything behind. Then, close to five o'clock with the streets crowded with people hurrying home from work, I made my way up in the direction of Christchurch. It was getting dark and a powerful wind was in my face all the way up the street. I got a bit of shelter when I turned left at the top of the street where the path grew wider. The pub was there opposite me, in a small sheltered alcove, a series of brass lamps lighting the sign above the front door—*The Clarence Mangan*.

The place was full of people escaping the responsibilities of their day, if they had any to escape, each table alive with earnest conversation, and people eagerly ordering drinks and food. Lesley was at a table over in the corner where he appeared to be shamelessly eavesdropping on the conversation of the people next to him.

"Lesley Ormonde?"

"Yes? Oh yes! How are you? Please, sit down, sit down ."

"I'd have arrived earlier if I knew that you were here already."

"Not at all, not at all. But I'll have a small brandy now if you're buying!"

The drinks arrived and a little later, some sand-wiches and a small jar of cockles for Lesley. He told me everything about his childhood and his mother and the special gift she'd been given so that she could foresee people's deaths ahead of time. He didn't say much about his own psychic abilities until I asked him what he felt when he was talking to the dead. He fell quiet for a moment before asking me whether I'd ever been in the crypt at Christchurch Cathedral—nodding in the direction of the front door. I told him that I had been. "Well," he said. I'd say you felt something when you were there, did you? Imagine that same feeling again but multiplied by a thousand."

It wasn't really his answers to my questions that satisfied my curiosity, even if I did ask him a lot of questions that afternoon, it was more that I felt I should remember every small detail of this meeting, right down to the cockles and this curious, misshapen person sitting opposite me. He became restless around seven o'clock and said he had to get ready for the show that night. I don't know whether it was the drink going to my head but I couldn't resist saying something about his crooked body.

"Do you know… Lesley, there's something about you, it's like you had a twin joined to you who has died and you have lived on. Is this your connection with the dead—is it your own twin?"

He produced a big white handkerchief from his breast pocket and blew his nose loudly, then wiped his nostrils fussily before putting the handkerchief away again.

"It's not a nice image. But you're a photographer, aren't you?"

"I am."

"Perhaps then, you only see what you want to see?"

I shook hands with him on leaving and he promised he'd come to Belfast at some stage so that we could take some photographs there. I could tell by the way that our conversation concluded that he hadn't taken my question badly. But, that said, I could never reach him at any of the phone numbers stated on the brochure. I left messages but never received any reply. You'd think, I said to myself, that someone who's able to talk to the dead could at least respond to the living—damn him! In the end, a secretary or agent of some sort answered the phone one day. He had no news from Lesley for me but he knew where he was all right: "Cheltenham. You definitely won't get him this week, he goes over every year."

"Is that allowed? You know—that he's gambling when he could be cheating away there?"

"How do you mean?"

"Well, couldn't he be getting tips from the dead about every race?"

"Oh no, he never wins much money on them but he's mad about the races."

"And does he do the lotto?"

"He does," he said, laughing loudly, as if he'd just thought of something rather innocent…"

"Yes, indeed, he does!"

Oliver Purcell

Every Friday afternoon I play football in a sports hall with a fluorescent green floor, one of those greens that you'd associate with a different planet. Not only is the floor interplanetary green, but there are powerful lamps in the ceiling that would blind you if you looked straight at them. On days when we've too many players, the game changes completely and becomes something else. You only have a split-second on the ball or someone takes it off you straight away. Twenty different processes happen in a nanosecond. Something else happens on occasions like this, which is as close to magic as can be imagined. Once your mind settles into the game, whatever fog that beset it previously lifts and the whole movement of play is transformed into a distant scene resembling an epic dance. People gliding over one another at speed, limbs and necks stretching wildly, rolling, probing and feinting, a frightening, trance-like expression on every face. It's as if all the desires and longing and melancholy are churning around in the cauldron of the subconscious, and there is no telling what sinister or evil thing it will bring forth. But if danger lurks there, there is also beauty, a beauty so alluring that you cannot but give yourself up to it completely.

Not that it's always like this, of course. Sometimes all there is, is the brutish, ungainly collision of bodies, mounds of flesh flopping around in sweat-drenched shirts, toes grinding and ankles twisting, great veins protruding like exposed electricity cables. But it's when I get a momentary glimpse of the epic football that I think of Oliver Purcell. For some reason, he has been in and out of mind over the past few months now too, like an intruder slipping in and out of a house before someone can waylay him. When we played football at school, Oliver was like a god to us, moving ghost-like through players and scoring goals like there was no one to oppose him. He was indomitable, invulnerable, immortal. And when you saw him in the middle of a match it was like being in the presence of something holy.

I hadn't seen Oliver for some time. No one knew where he was or what he was doing but what matter? Wherever he found himself, he was sure to be on top of the world, skimming across the surface of things, moving through people like the Holy Spirit. Nevertheless, I couldn't help noticing a certain unease about not seeing him around. It's not that I'd ever been great with him in the first place, but I would have seen him every now and then on the street. I was reluctant to go looking for him because I had never had much to do with him. Instead I thought of ways of bringing up his name in conversation every now and then, in an effort to glean information by directing the conversation to football or the old days at school. But no one had any news of him. I just needed to know what had happened to him and be done with it.

I continued searching for him discreetly on the Internet until I had to admit to myself that this search had nothing to do with Oliver Purcell but had more to do with myself. "I recognize," I thought to myself one day, "that the uncertainty all adults experience periodically is the cause of my 'missing' Oliver but I don't know what else to make of it. Perhaps it's the case that the subconscious must always walk guideless through a dark jungle, tripping and falling into holes all the while? Or is the subconscious guided in such a way that it conceals these from the rest of the mind and we fall into these holes by design?" I let these questions and others take root in the back of my mind in the hope that they'd answer themselves over time. It was in Autumn that year that I experienced all of this—if it was an experience at all—a question that wouldn't give way, like a rock in the road that couldn't be circumnavigated.

I spent nights listening to the clock hoping to inhabit the certainty of its rhythm. But it was no use. I was pushing against a great door that was too heavy for me to force open. I still played football weekly and every now and then, I sensed that same ethereal threshold as before. As for Oliver Purcell, he was a constant shadow on the margins of my perception. Then, shortly before Christmas, a small miraculous solstice occurred, letting in a chink of light. I recognized now that I'd been searching in the wrong place all along, looking for one big answer to Oliver Purcell, why I'd missed him, the subconscious in the jungle, the strange ethereality of football and the whole dizzying uncertainty. It was part of my upbringing to put my faith in one big answer, one movement, one God—and it wouldn't do me any more. I realized that I needed more than one god, whether I liked it or not, and that our ancestors had been right all along. We needed to recruit and appoint more gods: the God of Youth, the God of Light, the God of the Environment, the God of Justice, and the God of Football. Wasn't that what the old people did—didn't they pray to a whole variety of patron saints, each of which had their own unique responsibility and power? Whatever the case, it was well past time for us to end the monopoly of one god and replace him with the gods. It was time for us to deify every element of this great world, to give thanks for every small and blessed thing.

Something else happened that Christmas. On my way into the city centre on the bus one day, I glanced out at the crowd gathering into the shops buying presents. And there he was—his big bald head standing out amongst the milling crowd. He was wearing a long overcoat—of a style seldom seen in this country—and he was so tall that you'd have sworn he was standing on a wooden box ready to preach to the crowd. His hands were raised as if relating some adventure to the pair he was with, their eyes filled with wonder. He was a bit late but he was back amongst us again.

The Present Moment

Three years ago was when I first met Lucy. And when you meet someone like her for the first time, it's like you've just seen a ghost straight out of human history, you recognize them immediately and yet seeing them is to encounter a thundering, jolting shock. Imagine you were standing alone on a beach and you felt a hand on your shoulder, and you turned around to see Abraham Lincoln or Patrick Pearse standing in front of you—the living, breathing manifestation of them. Just imagine the shock you'd get! It's like waking someone who's been sleepwalking. For a short while afterwards, the chemistry that defines your mind and body is in turmoil so that a complete physical transformation ensues, and you're so frightened that you won't come up to the mark— so much so that you'd sell your soul for even some small hint of where your fate lies. And if you're lucky, and your desires are realized, you walk through a new door hoping never to return to the life you knew before. I'd hate for someone to undergo this more than once in their lives—but then who am I to say that such things don't happen to certain people on a regular basis?

All I know is that when it happened to me, it blew the head right off my shoulders. It causes you problems. You don't have time to think about all the people and things you are leaving behind forever. It's like you had to leave the country suddenly with no intention of ever returning. The web of life that you knew until then—that little map—it's all useless to you now.

You don't have time to end things properly or to say goodbye to people and the interactions you once had with them. You know what I mean—that conversation on the bus: "I don't see X any more these days, himself or herself—yeah, they're in love apparently." Maybe that's the real meaning of the story of Diarmuid and Gráinne—the flight from this life that follows the love between two people, the exile that is love. Maybe no-one was pursuing them at all and they were just evading the rest of the world. And there's no doubt that the pair who are in love seek out their own small secret hiding places everywhere they go, the same as Diarmuid and Gráinne did.

But it's not about hiding themselves away really; it's more that they're discovering one another's small and hidden redoubts—like a great army of invaders obliterating the last, small rebellious strongholds. Then, once they've surrendered every limb and all of the mind's secret hideouts to one another, the frenzy of love and "the couple" is born, two people as one, or as close as can be, that secret mysterious independent entity, a human simulation of the trinity but without its perfection.

You could say that this created difficulties for me! I'm a "young" man. A young man with a plan—one that I'm always revising, a plan that's sometimes torn up or left undeveloped when bouts of idleness or indifference come along. It's not worth outlining the main aspects of the plan here—the plan itself is unimportant—let's just say that I'm a young man who's always got something burning inside him. When I wake in the morning it's there in the patterns on the ceiling and when I go to sleep at night, it's staring in at me through the window. When I have a drink or two, I realize that the whole thing is ridiculous, and I laugh my head off and piss it up against the wall somewhere and move on.

But in the morning its back again like a slighted lover that I have to buy flowers for and win over again. I don't know how it all ends but I know this much— Lucy had no place in the "plan", and even if she did—you certainly weren't in it! But there's no use in talking. What's done is done and another door has closed behind me.

It's three years ago since I met Lucy, and it's just 20 minutes since she left to get the results of her test. That means I've one hour at most before this planet becomes unrecognizable to me again. One hour before I shed another skin and whatever I am now disappears for good. And that's what I'm at right this minute—providing an account of the person I am right now before this next radical transformation occurs.

It seems that this is the fate of "young" men these days—to be blown headlong by whatever comes along, directionless in the world. Some of us worse than others, some of us disappearing unexpectedly and others just falling by the wayside. There are certainly young men out there who are ploughing their own furrow and making their money for themselves, but it's the ones who've a conscience that I'm talking about, wherever they find themselves in the world, those ones whose conscience keeps them rooted like a pair of heavy concrete boots. But then again, was there ever a conscientious, young, man who felt entirely at home in this world? And herein lies the difficulty. What am I going to do about you if I don't know what do with myself? I've a friend and when he finds himself in a difficult situation like this, he starts packing his bags and getting ready for the airport—so he can get the next flight to London and from there on to Saudi Arabia—the place where he'll make his fortune. Saudi Arabia! This fellow would drink beer out of a pig-trough and needless to say, he's still here. He's never had it in him to leave—no more than myself. Whether I was always too stubborn-minded to leave my difficulties behind or whether I was a prisoner of my own mind, I never could anyway. And I wouldn't mind but the small blows that get to you in a place like this, I let them pile up and multiply the same as fleas on a dog so that in the end, I couldn't imagine life without them. Until recently it was politics that really got me going, but these days, it's something broader and at the same time closer to us too—this era we're living and all that goes with it. I had a dream a few nights ago that I haven't had since I was a child. A crowd of people are rushing up a giant staircase in a great building of some sort. Everyone's in a mad rush, myself included, trying to find my family or someone related to me, but none of them are there. Maybe it was the regular bomb scares we had as a child that were behind dreams like this, as it often happened that we were in a big department store somewhere in the city-centre—(or even at school a few times)—and everyone had to get out immediately. We were like refugees in our own country, driven from pillar to post, yet sweeping along together in a mindless stream.

Everything would be suddenly interrupted back then—whether it was Christmas shopping or a maths class, it didn't matter. On one such afternoon in early-summer, we were taken out of class and spent the day perched on a tall grassy mound outdoors, like a flock of sparrows. And whatever about the horrors of those days, there was a variety and unpredictability about life back then that no longer exists today. Strange as it may seem, we were protected from the dull monotony of modernity. It was as if as we were brought up in a little bubble of our own, one where the "national question" arose every morning in a cloudless sky and remained there until we fell asleep again at night. Others found this world difficult to understand and the more difficult they found it, the more it irked us that they were ignorant of how we lived. And as ugly and painful as this small subculture of ours could be, it steeled us in a way that we wouldn't bend or break. This is why we always stand like statues to the national anthem. And even if it makes little sense, I'd prefer to remain like this forever—to let that madness take over mind and body rather than yield to reason. I think this is why it's easier for me to explain who we are rather than who I am.

But right now, I'm waiting on Lucy, glancing out at the street. There are cars parked on either side of the street, beaded with great lusty droplets of rain like the lushest Amazonian leaves. And I have that feeling now that I get sometimes—that time is slipping past and there's no stopping it, and the key to existence is lost and the world doesn't care whether any of us lives or dies. This must be the estrangement of humanity from nature and I sense it strongly in this very moment. Maybe we only get the odd glimpse of it— as with the moon or the sun's eclipse—but I can tell that there's a star somewhere in the firmament that will displace me forever, and far from fearing it I am willing it to do so. Because my mind is afloat in that miraculous little moment, the act of consciousness that overcomes the chaos. I'm like one young person talking to another, someone else whose time has just begun.

www.ingramcontent.com/pod-product-compliance
Lightning Source LLC
LaVergne TN
LVHW011411080426
835511LV00005B/482